THIS BOOK BELONGS TO:

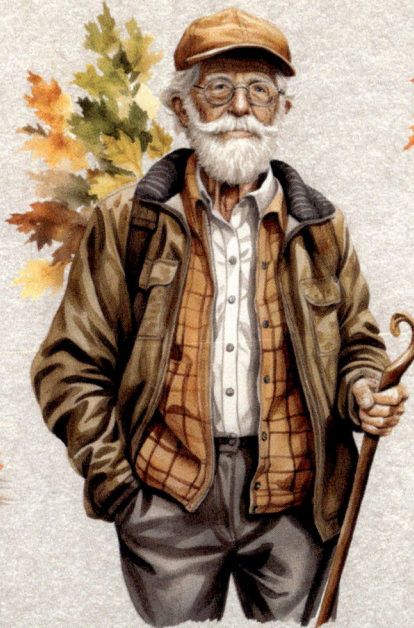

Thank you

THANK YOU FOR CHOOSING ONE OF MY COLLAGE BOOKS!
I KNOW YOU HAVE MANY GREAT CHOICES, BUT YOUR
PATRONAGE IS MY GREATEST SUPPORT!

PLEASE SHARE YOUR EXPERIENCE ON THE AMAZON

WE HOPE YOU HAVE AN ENJOYABLE AND MEMORABLE
COLLAGE JOURNEY THROUGH THIS BOOK!

PLEASE FOLLOW ME ON AMAZON!

SCAN ME

Kate Curry

BOOKSHELF

1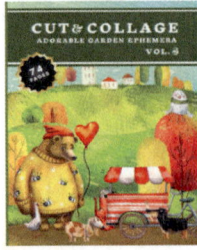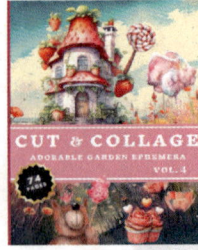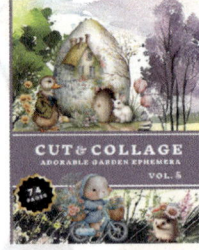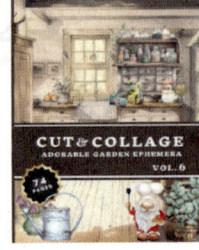

2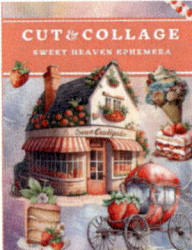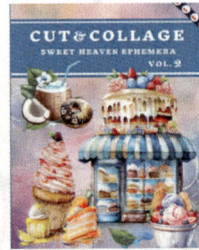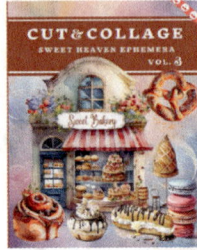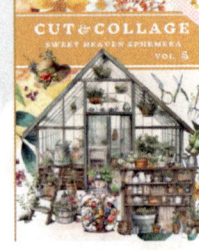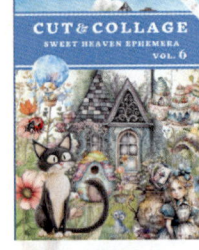

3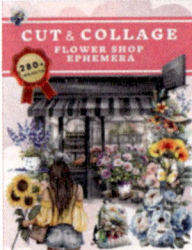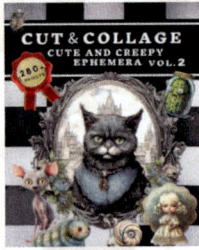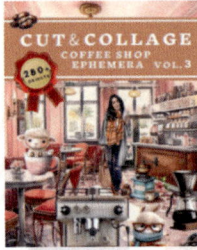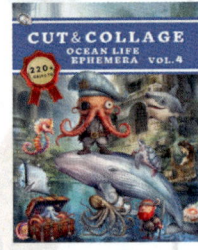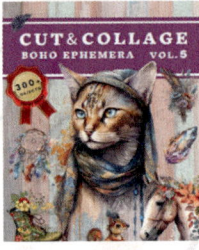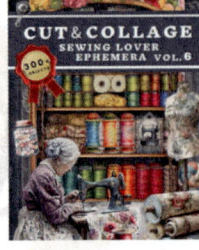

4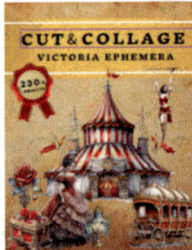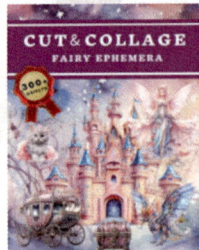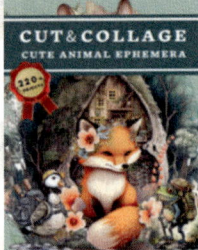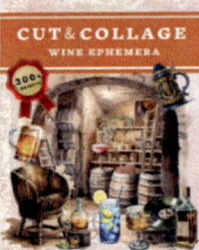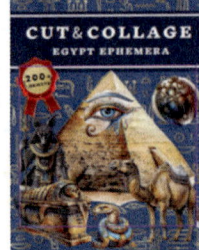

5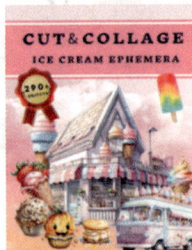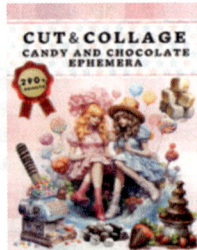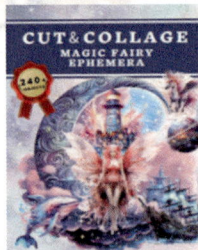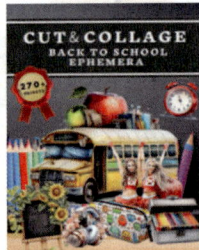

6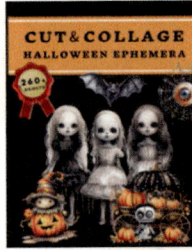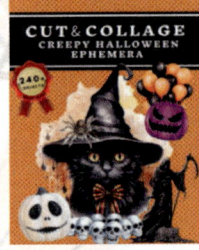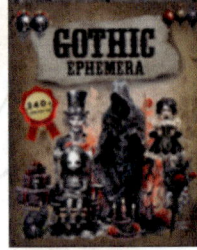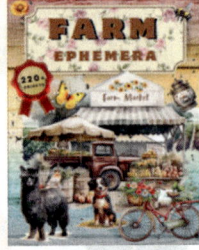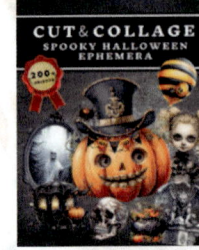

7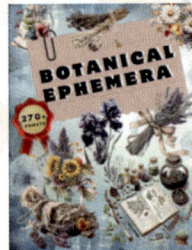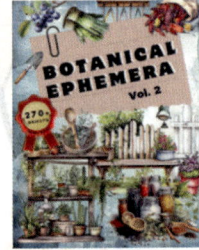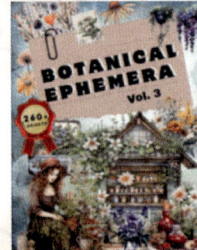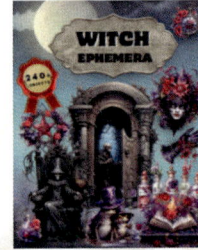

Made in the USA
Las Vegas, NV
17 June 2024